# I Dreamed A Dream
# SUSAN BOYLE

**Alfred**

Produced by
Alfred Music Publishing Co., Inc.
P.O. Box 10003
Van Nuys, CA 91410-0003
alfred.com

ISBN-10: 0-7390-6851-2
ISBN-13: 978-0-7390-6851-9

Image by Hugh Stewart, as appeared in the September 2009 issue of Harper's Bazaar U.S.

# CONTENTS

*The meaning behind each song by Susan Boyle*

## Wild Horses ...3

'Couldn't drag me away'. How can you help but be drawn in by this haunting theme. It conjures up memories of childhood amongst Council Estates, poverty and struggle in the first verse. Irony and bitterness. One of my personal favourites and an emotional release.

## I Dreamed A Dream ...10

Obviously from the musical 'Les Mis'. It's about a mother living in hard times. Very similar to my dream on a more personal level, of my 'life gone by' with mum who died at the age of 91 and whose "dream" it was that I should 'do something' with my life. Mum, this is for you.

## Cry Me A River ...16

About bitterness and anger as a relationship between a boy and girl has ended. A release of tension and a greater insight into the human condition. It's a Julie London song, with a lovely 1950s feel about it. I like that era. It seems so tame and innocent now.

## How Great Thou Art ...19

A hymn which has a great personal meaning to me as it reminds me of my friend who liked to sing this hymn in church.

## You'll See ...22

About determination, independence and the ability to show them what you are made of. Doubt sows disbelief. This is about turning this around. This song is a kind of beacon. A way of keeping going. My productive anger. My way of getting rid of the labels which have been unfair.

## Daydream Believer ...28

"The tears of yesterday don't mean a thing". There is happiness out there for everyone who dares to dream.

## Up To The Mountain ...33

Reassurance, Love and the ability to keep going no matter what 'slings and arrows of outrageous fortune' life throws at you. God is our Light.

## Amazing Grace ...39

About revelations. About finding your way. Everything was new to me. I was scared. Hope it's better. I know it can be with your continued support which I find both touching and humbling.

## Who I Was Born To Be ...42

Ambition, fate, call it what you will, but who was I born to be? Mum must have picked this for me.

## Proud ...48

This is about conflict between a parent and his son. The dilemmas most youngsters find themselves up against. My dilemma was finding my own identity – a conflict, if you like, with myself.

## The End Of The World ...53

Don't be silly! It's only the beginning! I want you all to enjoy some more!

## Silent Night ...57

Was first made public in Germany during a service on Christmas Eve. A touching hymn at Christmas – hope you like it.

# WILD HORSES

Words and Music by
MICK JAGGER and KEITH RICHARDS

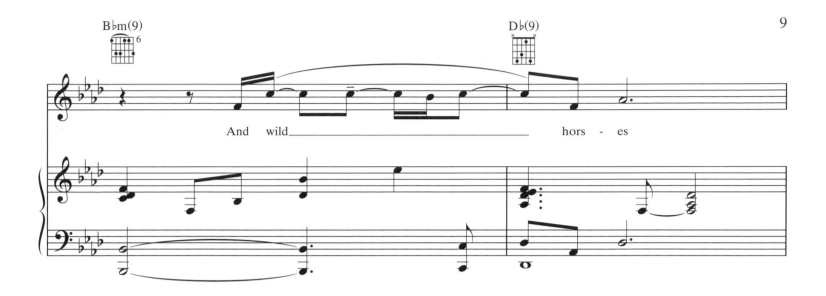

And wild_____ hors - es

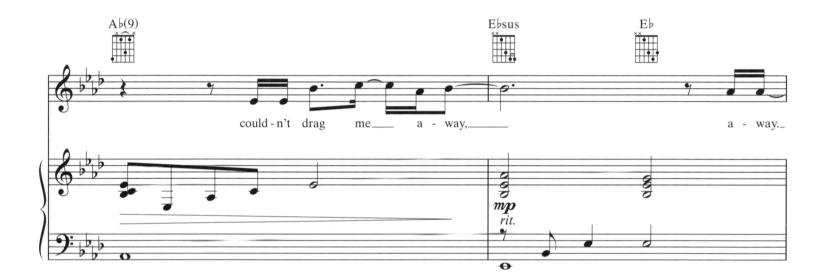

could - n't drag me____ a - way,_____ a - way._

**Freely**

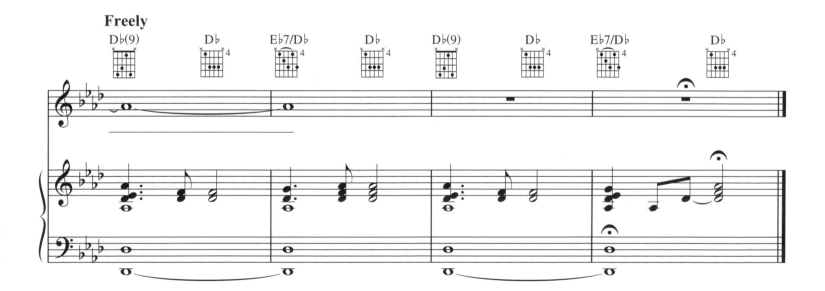

# I DREAMED A DREAM

### (from *Les Misérables*)

Lyrics by
ALAIN BOUBLIL, JEAN-MARC NATEL
and HERBERT KRETZMER

Music by
CLAUDE-MICHEL SCHÖENBERG

I dreamed a dream in time gone by,

when hope was high___ and life worth liv - ing.___

I Dreamed a Dream - 6 - 1
34615

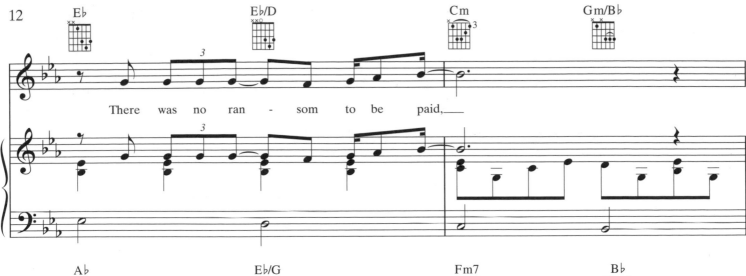

**More movement**

that we will live___ the years___ to - geth - er;___

but there are dreams___ that can - not be,___

and there are storms___ we can - not weath - er.

I had a dream___ my life would

# CRY ME A RIVER

Words and Music by
ARTHUR HAMILTON

# HOW GREAT THOU ART

Words and Music by
STUART K. HINE

# YOU'LL SEE

Words and Music by
MADONNA CICCONE and DAVID FOSTER

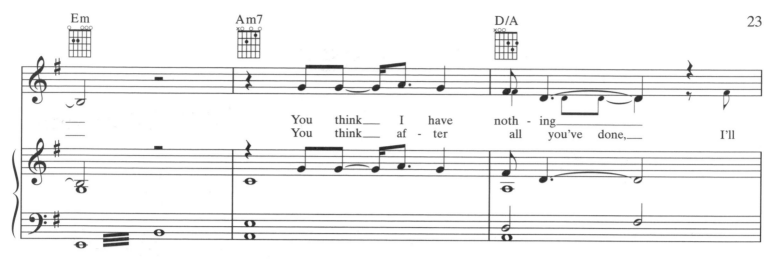

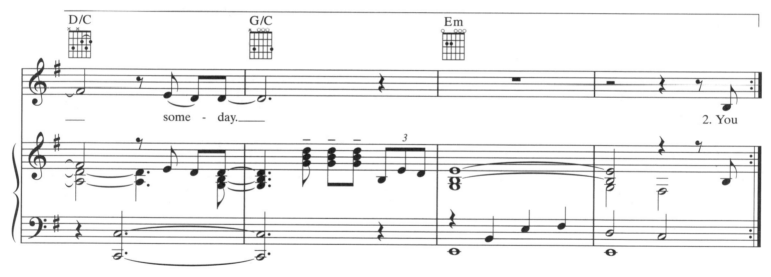

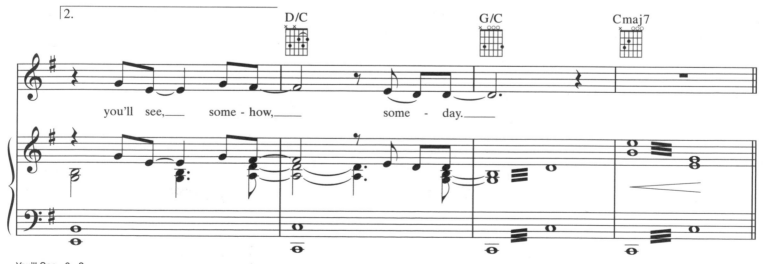

**Grandly**
*Chorus:*

**More rhythmically**

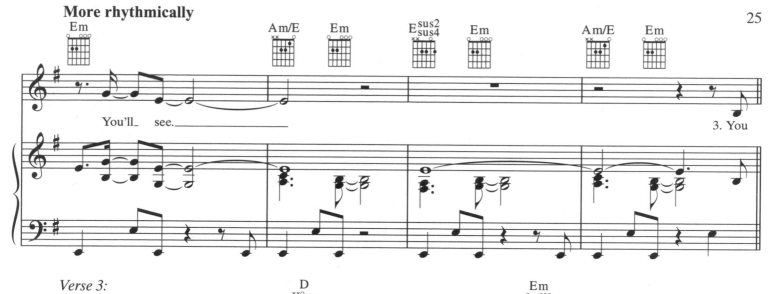

You'll see.

3. You

Verse 3:

think that you are strong, but you are weak; you'll see.

It takes more strength to cry, admit defeat.

I have truth on my side;

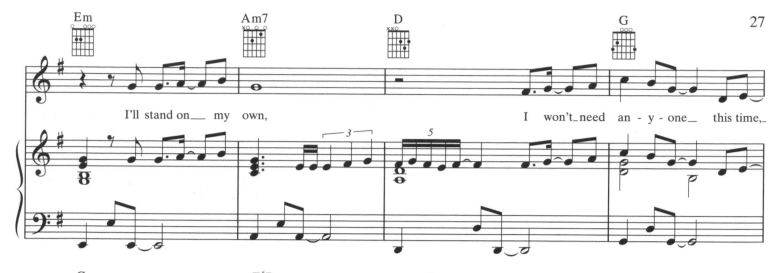

I'll stand on__ my own, I won't_ need an - y - one_ this time,_

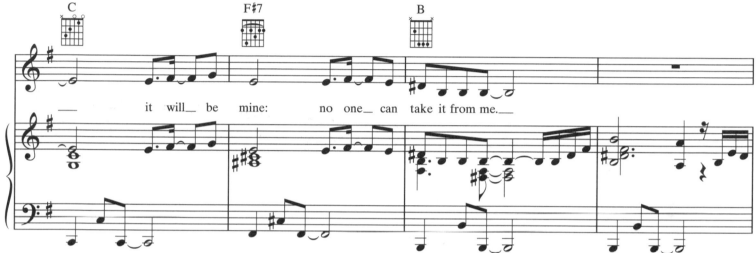

__ it will_ be mine: no one_ can take it from me.__

You'll_ see,_____ you'll see,_____

*you'll see.*

# DAYDREAM BELIEVER

Words and Music by
JOHN STEWART

**Gently and joyfully** ♩ = 104       *Verse 1:*

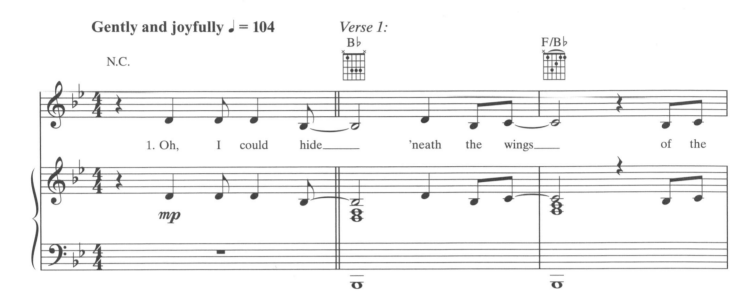

1. Oh, I could hide_____ 'neath the wings_____ of the

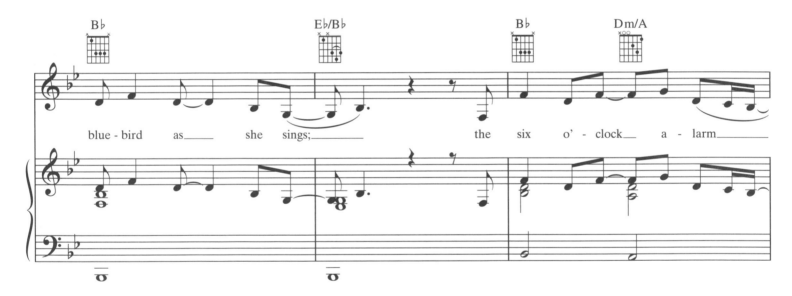

blue - bird as_____ she sings;_____ the six o' - clock__ a - larm

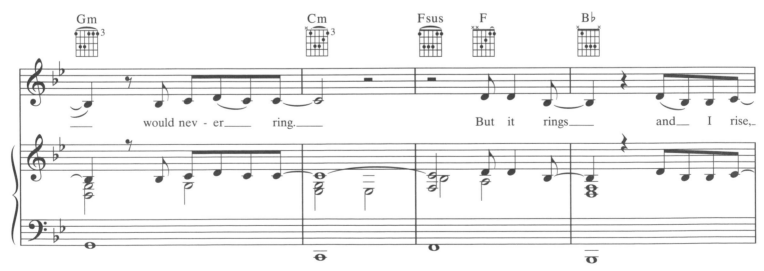

would nev - er_____ ring._____ But it rings_____ and_ I rise,

Daydream Believer - 5 - 1
34615

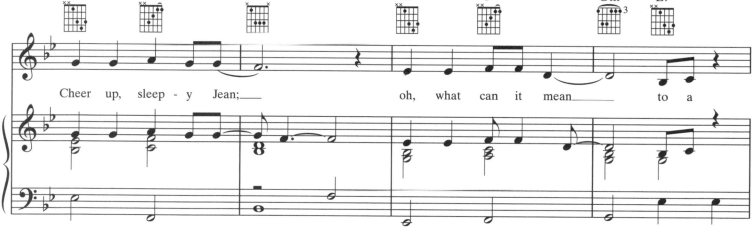

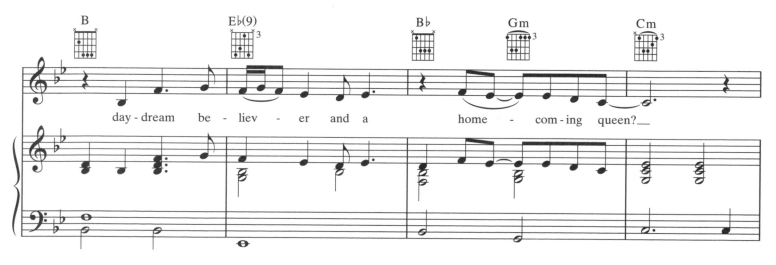

Daydream Believer - 5 - 2
34615

*Verse 2:*

once thought of me_____ as a white knight_ on_____ a steed;_

now you know_____ how_____ hap - py_____ I can

be. And our_____ good times_____ start and

end with-out dol - lar___ one___ to spend,___ but

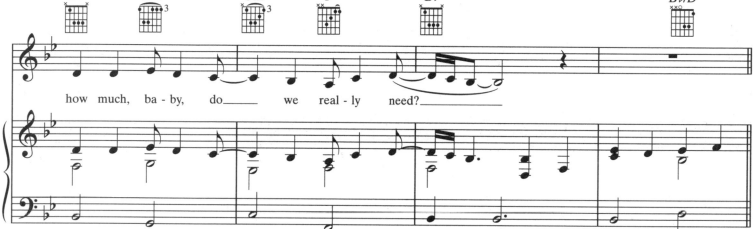

how much, ba - by, do___ we real - ly need?___

*Chorus:*

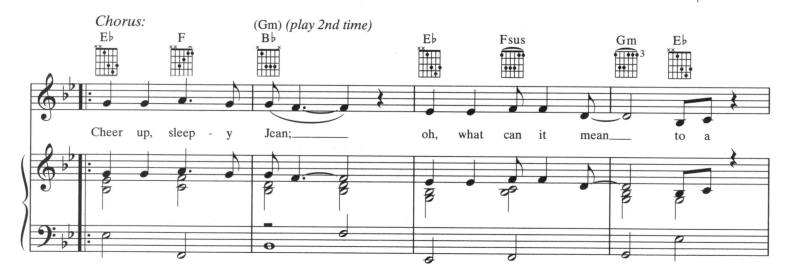

Cheer up, sleep - y Jean;___ oh, what can it mean___ to a

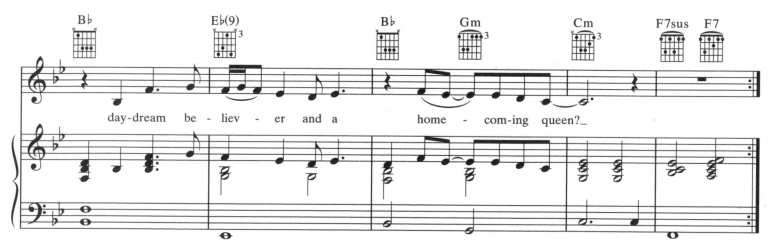

day-dream be - liev - er and a home - com - ing queen?_

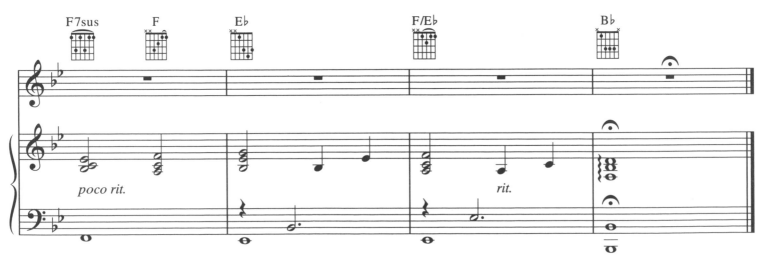

Cheer up, sleep - y Jean; _____ oh, what can it mean_____ to a

day - dream be - liev - er___ and a home - com - ing queen?___

poco rit.

rit.

# UP TO THE MOUNTAIN

## (MLK Song)

Words and Music by
PATTY GRIFFIN

*Original recording in B major.

Up to the Mountain - 6 - 1
34615

# AMAZING GRACE

Traditional,
Arranged by STEVE MAC and DAVE ARCH

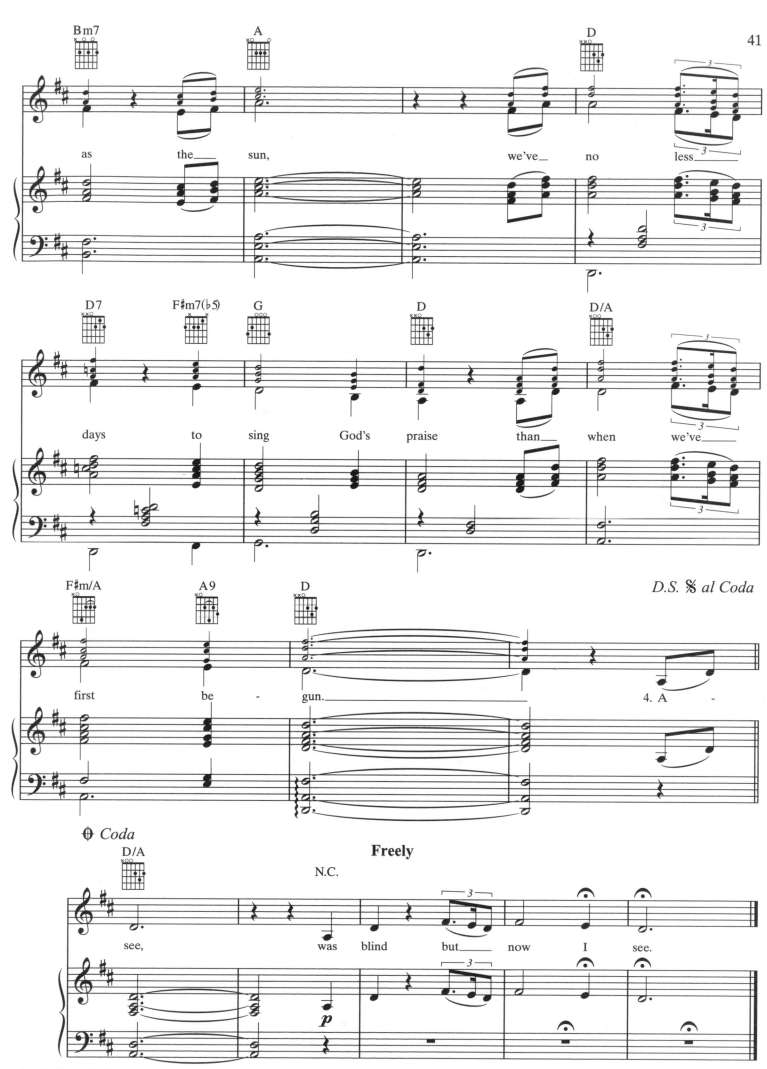

# WHO I WAS BORN TO BE

Words and Music by
AUDRA MAE BUTTS, JOHAN FRANSSON,
TOBIAS LUNDGREN and MIKAEL LARSSON

*Chorus:*

may_____ not_ know the an - swers,_ I can fi - n'lly say_____ I'm free. And if the ques - tions_ led me here,_____ then_ I am who_____ I was born_____ to be._

# PROUD

Words and Music by
STEVE MAC, WAYNE HECTOR
and ANDY HILL

*Verse 2:*

Say I'm some-one in your eyes;_____ that's all I want-ed to_____ be.

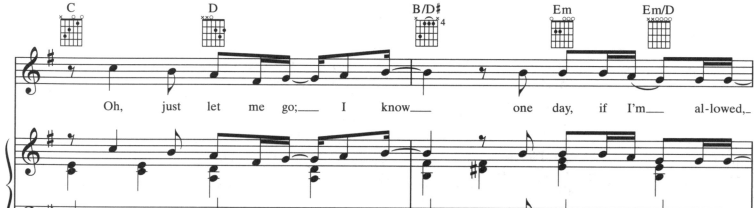

Oh, just let me go;_____ I know_____ one day, if I'm_____ al-lowed,_

if I'm_____ al - lowed,_____ one day I'll make_ you

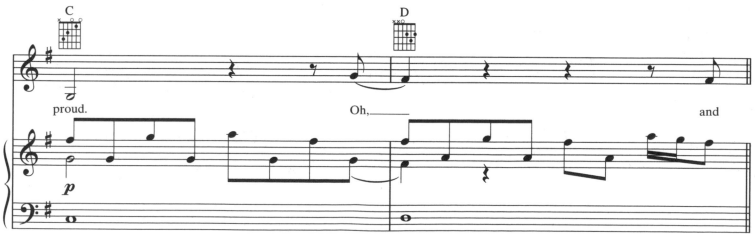

proud. Oh,_____ and

# THE END OF THE WORLD

Words and Music by
ARTHUR KENT and SYLVIA DEE

**Innocently** ♩. = 52

Why___ does the sun go on

shin - ing?___ Why___ does the sea rush___ to the shore?

Don't they know___ it's the end___ of the world, 'cause you don't love me___ an-y-

*Original recording is in B major.

The End of the World - 4 - 1
34615

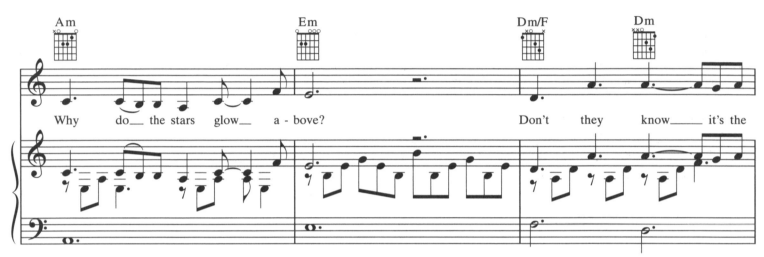

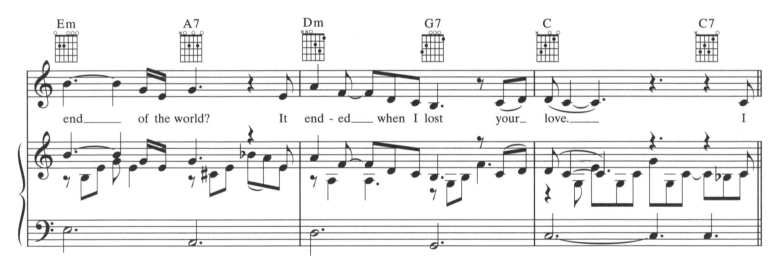

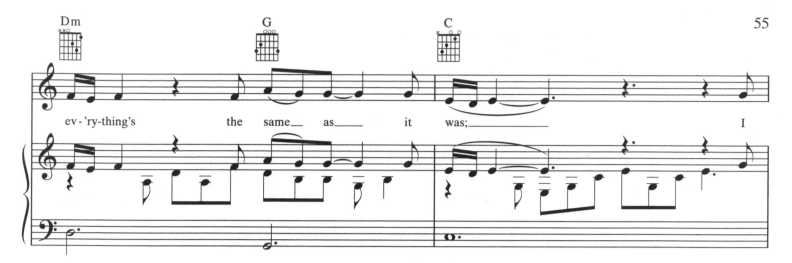

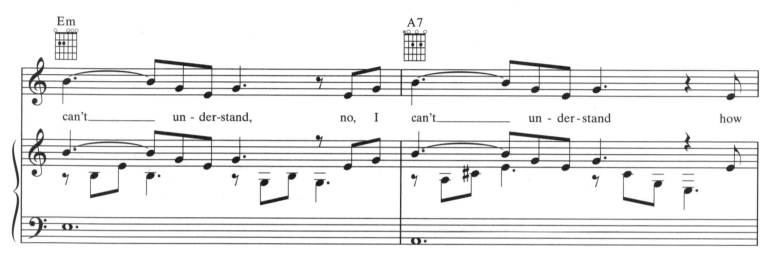

The End of the World - 4 - 3
34615

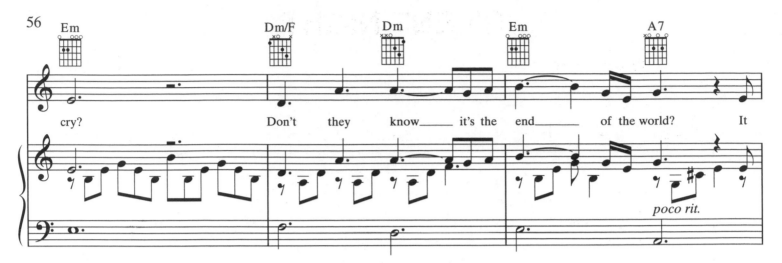

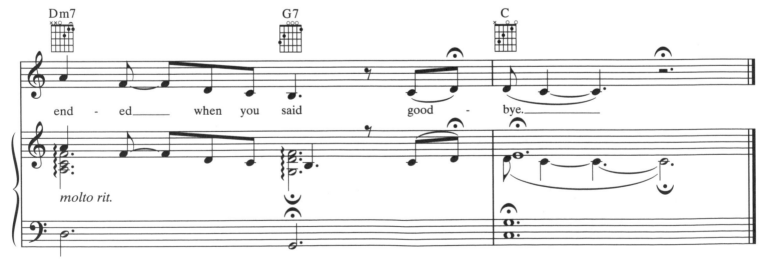

# SILENT NIGHT

Traditional,
Arranged by STEVE MAC

# Susan Boyle

There are unlikely stories. There are fairytales. There are dreams that come true. Susan Boyle's story is all of these and more, and one that instantly stirred emotions all over the world. Driven to succeed despite years of rejection, Susan is proof that perseverance and single-mindedness can shine in a world that is too-often quick to jump to conclusions and allow cynicism to prevail.

Susan's parents, Patrick and Bridget Boyle, were of Irish stock along with many others who sought a future in Scotland. Theirs was a tight-knit community in Blackburn near Edinburgh. The youngest of nine children, Susan was deeply devoted to her mother. "When I was a baby they told my parents not to expect too much of me because I had a slight disability. I didn't make friends very easily—I couldn't trust anybody, and when I did try to speak to people they made fun of me. So my only escape from all that really was music." There is no doubt that Susan was determined to sing. After all, it is that which makes her special. She took singing lessons, attended Edinburgh Acting School, and took part in the Edinburgh Fringe. Throughout her life, Susan sang wherever she could—entering many talent competitions, but mainly singing in her local pub where they had karaoke, and regularly in her local church.

But the 21st of January 2009 changed everything—Susan became an overnight success at 47 years of age. "I will never forget it," she says in her distinctive Scottish brogue. On that day, she had stepped onto the stage of the Scottish Exhibition and Conference Centre in Glasgow to audition for *Britain's Got Talent*, and the initially sceptical panel and audience were spellbound as soon as she started to sing "I Dreamed a Dream."

"I got a standing ovation and then the judges stood up. It was exhilarating and it was amazing. In fact, I said at the time it was bloody fantastic." In her own unpredictable fashion, during three and a half minutes of television gold, Susan had fashioned a new kind of fame.

Sir Cameron Mackintosh—possibly the most influential theatre producer in the world—describes that night: "From the first moment she started to sing 'I Dreamed a Dream,' I was just on the edge of my seat going, 'Wow can she sustain it?' And for some reason, the lyrics of that song seemed to epitomise what she wanted—her own dream of life, indeed her own life experience."

It is, perhaps, Susan's fragility that endears her to her audience most as they will her to succeed. Piers Morgan, who was on the judging panel along with Simon Cowell, said, "It was spellbinding. It was one of those moments when your spine starts to tingle. It was amazing." Simon said, "That was the moment where I thought, if she can hit the chorus, this song is going to change her life forever. I could feel it." Susan, as ever, was self-deprecating about her performance and the response to it: "A woman who went on with mad hair, bushy eyebrows, and the frock I was wearing had to be noticed. Come on!"

Nothing could have prepared Susan for what happened next. The global village that is the instant communication power of the Internet exploded with the news of Susan's triumph. YouTube immediately became Susan's window to the world, and she enjoyed global fame almost overnight. Not all of this initially sat easily with Susan, and she had moments of self-doubt and the thought that, at any time, her chance could disappear.

After *Britain's Got Talent*, Susan immersed herself in the making of her debut album, aptly called *I Dreamed a Dream*. In the studio, veteran producer Steve Mac immediately recognised the delicate beauty and quality to her voice. She fashioned the record over two months, picking songs that resonated with her, that touched something within that she felt ready to unleash through music. "It was important that I could feel everything I was singing," she says.

A disarming mix of the sacred (she says her faith is her backbone) and the secular, every moment on the album is moving. It is pitched exactly within the framework of the year she has enjoyed and, at well-documented times, endured. It is a collection of classics and original material that reflects the life of the woman that is Susan Boyle.

Her rousing rendition of Madonna's "You'll See" is a riposte to the children who picked on her in the playground. The original composition "Who I Was Born to Be" is an astonishing testament to self-belief against some startling odds. Yet, when she dreams, we dream too. Because of her uncanny knack for picking a song at that very first audition that was so perfect for her tale, she has become synonymous with the word "dream." Her flawless album rendition of "I Dreamed a Dream" may come as no surprise, but it still manages to stun every individual hair on the back of your neck. As Sir Cameron Mackintosh said, "No one's actually owned 'I Dreamed a Dream' until Susan Boyle captured our hearts."

Susan's appearances on *Dancing with the Stars* and her rendition of the Rolling Stones' "Wild Horses" heightened expectations in advance of the release of her album. However, no one could have anticipated what happened next. The album was released in late November 2009 and went straight to No. 1 in the United States and the United Kingdom, as well as in many countries around the world. So many firsts attach to this album and so many superlatives have been expressed about it. *I Dreamed a Dream* is the fastest-selling UK debut album of all time, and in the U.S., the album sold 700,000 copies in its first week, the best opening week for a debut artist in over a decade.

We all share in the rollercoaster life of Susan because so many of us can identify with her. She shows us the light at the end of the tunnel and the silver lining in every cloud. She is sure to entertain us for many years to come with her extraordinary gift.